What do You Say to an Ugly Baby?

Gary K. Wright
3/23/2012

Dedication

I dedicate this book to David, Amy, Katalina, Liliana, and "Baby David"

They are all beautiful and kind. They have a family that works hard and works together.

Each child is a dream come true, for parents who create a place of love, both in their hearts and home.

Thank you so much for including me amongst the members of your family.

Lovingly, Uncle Gary

Contents

What Do You Say To An Ugly Baby?

~

What do you say to an ugly baby?

"How sweet!" or "How lovely her hair bow!" Or "Wow! I bet he grows up to be a linebacker", etc.

We each have a moment in our life when we take a look at what we hope will be the epitome of beauty when a proud new Mother or Father uncovers the face of their little darling.

You are not allowed to bark or whinny or howl at the moon.
You must always say something discrete and appropriate; unless, of course, the child truly is a vision of loveliness. Then by all means, pour on the compliments.

Remember, though, too much of a good thing is just that...too much. If you over gush the parents my not think you are being sincere. Then they start to doubt if their "cuddily-wuddily" is really "…uggily buggily…"

You have an obligation to maintain the status quo and allow those parents to know they have propagated and brought forth a child deserving of admiration, one that should not learn to live off the adoration of others throughout their lifetime but learn by accepting with grace, a well-deserved compliment.

Imagine with me for a moment that the couple before you are some of your truest friends and you have all waited a lengthy period of time to have this bundle of joy presented to you. Cute or ugly?

This is a tale of how one might proceed:

"Hey, you two? What's this?"

They beam…smiles from ear to ear…*the hand* comes to the edge of the blanket and that dreaded moment arrives.

.

As though time was suspended, you see *the hand* grasp the coverlet and then move it aside, as if in slow motion, and you prepare yourself.

You swallow several times, slight little swallows, hopefully almost imperceptible. You dare not seem too nervous, no big gulps, those are a dead give-away that your fears may be fulfilled when your eyes meet the face of your best friends' newborn infant.

You look up in the face of the guy with whom you went through elementary, middle and high school together. You graduated with him second in the class at college and you serve as a newbie with him on the Alumni Committee.

You started with the same company and he passed you up into management just two years after your initial introduction to the shoots-and-ladders that take you up and down with said company. You have always been there for him and supported him in the life you share as buddies, bros, et al.

You were Best man at his wedding last year and best friends forever. He was just over at your place to pick you up last week to take you out to the baseball game…your team won. You took him out to celebrate the victory!

He has always been there for you and you for him.

This kid had better be pretty!?!?!?!

What if it isn't. Matter of fact, What kind is it?
Oh, I forgot ask. I did. I can't remember. Is it a
"blue baby "or a "pink baby"?
Why do things like this have to be so difficult?
What if I say something stupid about the kid.

The Crux

There… is the crux of the whole thing. We put ourselves in real jeopardy by not knowing what to say. We fear creating a situation where you must back out of a statement you started but realized was not appropriate, or that sounded dull, lame or dumb.
You languish in the unpleasant sweat of your own making because you didn't pay attention to some of the things on which you are about to be tested.

The payoff could be great! On the other hand, you could be cut off in the disaster that would be wrong words; falling, stumbling, stagnating, befuddling, bemusing…in all actuality saying the wrong thing could ruin ~ end your friendship.

But if you don't say something, you might offend his sweetheart and bride of only 14 months.

It was a great wedding, as far as weddings go. You got to stand up with him, smile at the cute women (wink, flirt, blow kisses), be admired by a few and you got to drink. You drank A LOT as a matter of fact. And it was paradise!

You got to speak…that toast, Wow! Whatever it was you said sure made an impression on everyone, especially the brides' family.

I bet you thought they already knew all those things about the other women in your best friends' life. All those stories about when everyone thought you and he were off on some business adventure and…well, whatever.

The bride appreciated it though. Didn't she? Well, I can't honestly recollect.

Here she is, right in front of you with her new lovely; a product of their love, now clutched in her gentle Mommy-type arms. A little star sent to Earth to shine brightly and make their lives more complete. That's what they say, don't they?

Why does it have to be like this? Why didn't someone just write a simple little book and give it to you or read it to you and it would make all of this easy, simple, fearless.

But, alas, that did not happen.

Now you have to go it alone. You have to be the big brother, the uncle, the god-father and buck up your senses and figure out what it is that you will say when that formidable hand completely tears the shroud away and there in plain sight, for YOU to see, is their child.

Now it is your time to flash a smile and eloquently state your true feelings about the enchanting bliss which is steadied, hands out, exerting pressure on you to extricate the child from her Mothers' grip and proliferate in a tone and a language that signifies your truth, as you see it (literally).

Explicatives of grandeur are warranted. They will illustrate the arrival of this child into your world as well as that of your friends. Make them words so festive and yet inspirational that they will be treasured forever by the happy couple.

Remember they are new to all of this and they wait with baited breath to find out how you too adore and cherish their contribution to the love in their lives.

The moment is here. You open your mouth. You have given it great thought. Trillions of ideas have shot into and out of your mind. Your sweating brow is now somewhat less obvious. You reach out, take the child in your hands and you say,

"Cute, huh?!"

What? What did you just say? That is not what you really meant to say. Well, maybe it didn't sound too bad, you know or maybe it did sound all that bad?" What if it did?

Stop! Think Man!

You saw the look in their eyes before you said it, right? You really really thought about it, right? Right!

You're thinking: "She's not a bad looking kid…for a newborn and all. Sure she has red hair.

Kinda wrinkly and all, though.

I don't know what those splotches are on her head and face. Little bumps, too.

But what happens with those little hands. Man they grabbed at me. How does a kid that size have such a strong grip? At least she has all her parts, well, you know, hands and fingers, stuff you can see right off…nose, eyes; same color eyes as her Dad.

Wow! She's a light weight. Had no idea she would be so small. Smells good for a kid, too!

Kinda clean and soft. Ever touch anything so soft before?

Hey, she's looking straight at me. Whoa! a smile. This is something. I never thought about a kid that size being able to smile. No teeth. She's gotta do some growing, needs teeth.

Look at this; too…she's starting to fall asleep. Geez, I was just holding her and she starts to nod off. Fun! I wonder if she snores. No, can't, too cute to snore.

I think I might like this Uncle stuff. Wonder if she will always smell this good. Nice smile."

As you look back into the faces of the doting Mom and Dad, you see tears of acceptance rolling down their cheeks. Yeah, even your best buddy has to wipe away the signs of his pride and joy. He cherishes you as a friend; he is truly seeing his own little girl in the arms of his best friend. He hugs his wife, they twitter about something, only spoken in baby-talk as he reaches out and asks if they should take the baby back.

There is a bit of hesitation. You know there will other times to hold your new *niece*. Things won't be the same with you and your best friend, from now on. There will be an added force in your relationship and you will spend less time together. But somehow you understand the value of the new dimensions of friendship. You are, after all, a part of it.

So what did you say to an ugly baby? Anything! The truth is in the old saying, "Beauty is in the eyes of the beholder"

Saying Anything

My Mom always said, "If you can't say anything nice,
don't say anything it at all!"

But sometimes, things have to be said. It is not clear why, though. But there is this thing down deep inside our gut that forces its way out and clambers to be spoken. Matter-of-fact, the more you try to suppress it the louder it is when the thing is finally blurted out.

There becomes so much pressure from the need to say a thing that whether or not it is reasonable has nothing to do with it, the spring is wound too tight and it POPS OUT and is thus distributed, justly or not, all over everyone in hearing distance.

This is the sad consequence of holding a thing in. When it is the truth, especially, the release can be very messy for those who are within the vicinity.

I don't mean, in any way, that a thing should be kept in. If we were not so frugal with our emotions about a thing…especially when it is a sincere and pure emotion, we should rightfully express it with a clear conscience.

Naturally there follows a… HOWEVER…

We are simply taught to keep certain things to ourselves. If you ever have had to quash the openness of a young child who has seen an overweight person or someone who is physically different, and loudly proclaimed that difference to all in ear shot, you understand what the "however" is for.

There are just sometimes we fear the results of our words, or the words of others. We feel the humiliation through a deep empathy wishing we had not heard it or it had not been heard by that someone (or anyone) as it may have even come out of our very own mouth. It did not sound the way it was meant, it sounded wrong. How convoluted is that!!!!

~~~~~~~

There are moments in our lives when we simply do not know what to say. Our mouths are shut whether by fear of saying the wrong thing or saying too much and sounding insincere; or saying the right thing, but not enough, leaving the listener wanting to know if you will ever finish the sentence you started.
~~~~~~~

It is something that we each must face when the time comes. It is necessary to understand that no matter which approach you take it will never truly define what it is you really meant, whether stated or implied.

Have you got a clue as to what is really required in any given situation? No, probably not. This is the exact reason for this bit of literature! To help you get through the trying times. Words fail us and we look embarrassingly humiliated by either our words or the lack of them. What have you insinuated?

One of our greatest fears is to be publically humiliated and I could safely assume that each and every one of us has either had it happen to us or somehow carefully, thoughtfully, artfully dodged having it happen to us.

The enigma of having been put into a predicament where we felt so alarmed and transduced into thinking that anyone around us would find us perfectly ridiculous - for our reaction or verbiage - accounts for the deep seeded knowledge that we would not dare put our self in another position that might call down upon us another calamity like the one we had previously encountered.

We learn by experience, whether our own or seeing it happen to another. Thank goodness we learn!

There is a consequence to all things. We eventually learn what those consequences are and try to attain or avoid them, as necessary.

Lil D

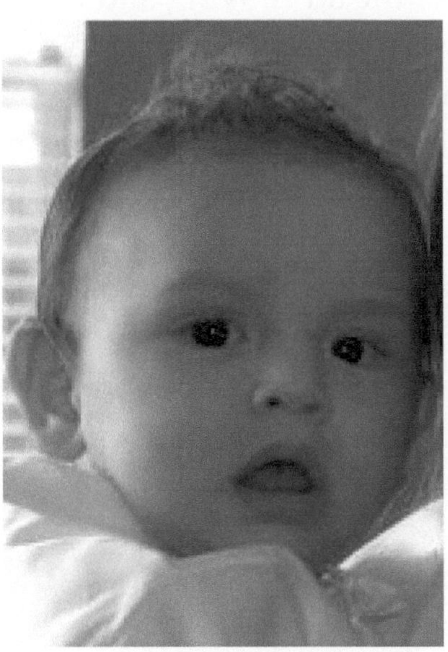

Humiliations

Who dares to fart in church? No one! Even though we can all smell that someone did, there is not a soul in the congregation that will admit to it. So we pass it off to the excitement of the holy ghost and low-and-behold we have another incident where blame filters out the door (and the perpetrator) along with the odiferous presents that recently made itself known to us.

When you were a kid in chemistry, did your teacher ever do the "light the sulfur" trick. They do that to show you that even though we do not see the air moving and the molecules crashing, that something so foul smelling which happens in one part of the room will eventually be noticed by everyone in all parts of the room due to air currents molecular movement, etc..

Sounds like regular life to me. When you least want someone to find out about the secret you have the sooner they all do and judge you accordingly.

Here's something to think about...*judgment*.

We have in our holy writ the verse that says, "Judge not lest ye be judged". Now that has always meant to me, that you just take who or what a person is in stride and allow it to be.

Whatever happens in conjunction with that person is just a part of the whole and there is no reason to get upset with them. In other words, we accept our self and others as we truly are!

Wish that were also the truth. But there are simply times when I do not live by that terrific moral code. I see, smell or hear someone and immediately I jump to the stereotype that person actions or comments solicit in me.

Now, I am talking about a person who is like a Lumberjack, Street Hooker, Gay, Red Neck, Less Educated Person, Jock, of a different ethnicity, etc., etc., etc. You follow my train of thought here, right?

We all have had life experiences that have shown us that certain types of people think, act and talk in similar ways. That is how stereotypes begin and are perpetuated.

The problem is, sometimes we take them to heart and define all of our acquaintances by the same delusionary rules.

Remember in the English languages there are the rules and the exceptions. The rotten part about it is that sometimes the exceptions outweigh the rules. Some words sound the same but have entirely different meanings. Some words look the same but are pronounced differently. Some words are different but have the same meaning.

(Now, how is that possible? I don't really know. I did not cultivate the English language; I only learned it as a byproduct of growing up in the U.S.A.)

Not only that, but I have dialectic influences to deal with. As I grew older I heard people who have been raised in other parts of the country or maybe even the part of the Pacific Northwest where I was reared, and I hear things either not familiar or familiar and no longer used by me. I have replaced certain terms that were once quite common to me. I have lived all over America and found very interesting speech anomalies. I do not mean to infract that I think they are wrong, just different from others.

The Buddhists have a belief that there is nothing right or wrong, just different. That is a logical way of thinking about many things here on planet Earth.

That leaves it wide open for a multiplicity of interpretations, to whatever degree. Even what we consider horrendous crimes would then be understood as only a part of what makes up the person committing said crime as well as the recipient of that criminal action.

The murderer and the victim then are neither right nor wrong, but they - simple and plain – exist as **being**. We just ARE! What happens to us is all part of what and who we are, thus it can be neither right nor wrong.
Things happen, and so it is.

We'll back up to square one.
What do you say to someone who readily admits to be an alcoholic? A Prostitute, Gay, a non-working Mom, a Senator, a Dentist, a Biochemist, an Astronaut, a Waitperson, a Son, a Dad, a Pedophile, a Writer, a Boxer, a Construction worker…
you know this list could go on for most all the book, so, I will stop for all our sakes.

You can see that we all have different feelings and pictures in our minds about who these people are and how they have affected our lives in the past and present. It is how we view them through our emotions that dictate how we react to them.

If our reaction is based on fear, then we need to try to change that; if it is based on loving acceptance, well, I am not sure you would want to change it.

I feel that is the answer to this whole thing. We need to understand that our lives are subject to very strong emotions and we react to events in life with only these two emotions. One is fear; the other is love...so says the New Age writer Neale Donald Walsch.

Based on his ideology, I have to insist that it seems so darn logical that if we overcome our fears, then living with others that are different will become less of a challenge and more of a pleasure in our future relationships.

I will never forget the time my Mom and I were in a mall and we were people watching. We had been sitting for several minutes when we decided to get up and travel down the mall for other means of entertainment.

I had worked with the developmentally disabled for eleven years, so few things were a surprise to me, but there was a woman who quickly came toward us to say hello. She startled me so, that I yelled at her to get away.

She was hideous looking to me, deformed facial features like the guy in the movie *MASK.* I felt over protective toward my Mom and kinda let out a yelp for myself too. She saw that in my face, heard it in my voice and I was humiliated to think that she had to experience a lack of compassion from me with such an impact, I still feel very bad for hurting her feelings.

I could see it in her eyes. Having said this, it was a great lesson for me to be aware of who and what is around me at all times. So, I am neither frightened like that again, nor do I react too strongly.

I know you are probably saying that you would have done the same thing. But we each learn in a different way. So this lesson was mine, to create in me a more tender loving heart and a keener eye to my whereabouts.

I appreciate your empathy, but it really made me think I was not all I thought I could have been in that aspect of my life. So I worked on first chastising myself for being such an asshole and then hoping that she eventually learned that not all people are assholes like me. I wanted, years later, to relive that episode and befriend her, if only for a moment, so she would know how deeply sorry I was.

I have done it dozens of times in my heart, but naturally it never happened in real time. "The present is based on the past". I like that saying. We must never forget it or we're bound to repeat it.

TRUTH

One of the reasons for this book is because I know the truth of that saying. I want others to understand that we learn from our mistakes, if that is what they truly are. We need to live in a "right-now" perception where each one and everything we once were has helped to create the composition that we now are.

Metaphorically speaking we are a balanced symphony presenting itself in beauty and splendor for others to see and hear…however our perception of our self may be that we are a composition yet unnamed and ill-composed?

I can't say that either one is truly accurate. Because I feel there are times when I am neither and both, simultaneously.

I am not a finished work, but not a poorly constructed composition either.

It is like being able to go to the rehearsals and see that some things need to be more practiced, thus repeated until excellence is achieved;

while others are fine, needing only to be put in their proper perspective in the piece.

Supplemental information would infer that we are never either. We are always unfinished, but never poorly in tune. We are neither right nor wrong in our presentation of our unified whole as a person. We are never complete, that's why we come back time and again to the refresher course called humankind (on this Earth). We will continually try to tune our instrument and make the most beautiful music of the soul that we can. I don't know how that is accomplished, exactly, but is that working for you?

Well, you can guess that if it were not working, we would have perished long ago. We live for the ideals that, for whatever abides within each of us, that we need to continue to create a story line that will help us write the full anthology of who and what each of us is, both here and now; in the future and past.
We realize we have a relationship with the past from which we can't seem to let go.

I am not talking about the simple form of not repeating our mistakes in society. I am talking about where we came from originally and why we are here right now.

I am not in any way shape or form trying to get into the philosophical idealisms of the origins of life, etc. I am just making the comment, that we all seem to enter into that arena of thinking "from whence we came", sometime in our life so we need to decide for ourselves whether or not it is pertinent to our present existence.

Reality

I have recently been thinking about why I continued to work so many years, 42 in all. Not just that I needed to make money to help out in the household, but why during a time when physical pain and stress increased to such a degree that at the end of a work day I could barely walk or stand. Did I still feel I owed it to my employers to do my very best, even though it causes me great agony when the day is over?

I even found myself hiding the muscle pain or limp when I worked, so those around me would not either pity me nor condemn me for being less of a person than what I was.

Did you get all that? Do you understand that sometimes we do stuff because of our perception of what we think others might be thinking or saying about us? When truthfully - it is only in our mind.

If we have not been open or honest about how we feel or what we think we need to do, thus hiding reality, then there is no answer.

Answers only come once a question or statement has been posed within the realm of our individual ability to understand. So, what did I learn about this? I have not processed it all, not by this time, anyway. I would not have brought it up though, if it was not being processed and an answer being brought forth from within me.

I whole heartedly believe that things happen in due time – a correct time. There is a verse that says, "*to everything there is a season, and a time to every purpose under heaven; A time to be born and a time to die; a time to plant, and a time to pluck up that which is planted; a time to kill and a time to heal; a time to break down, and a time to build up; a time to weep and a time to laugh; a time to mourn, and a time to dance; a time to cast stones, and a time to gather stones together; a time to embrace, and a time to refrain from embracing; a time to get , and a time to lose; a time to keep and a time to cast away; a time to rend and a time to sew; a time to keep silence and a time to speak; a time to love and a time to hate; a time for war, and a time for peace.*" Ecc. 3:1

Now, I tell you, that much of what we live by in our person code of ethics is (or was) based on the interpretation of those verses?

We have ideas, ideals, philosophies, dogma, rules, regulations, honor codes and an abundance of other guideline-esque life directing verbiage in our hearts buried from years gone by. There are things that dwell in our souls that are a part of us that we can't truly define except when the outcome of our actions has been shown.

There are so many things in us, deep seeded, that we learned as children and we took to be the absolute truth for our self. Thus we have lived by the moral code that developed out of it. We have practiced it all our lives. And this does not mean that it is all good.

We now live in a world that is so convoluted in its multiplicity of religious and benign practices that there are too many gaps, too many things to question, too many falsehoods that to seek them out only gets you embroiled in a tangle of misconceptions that can never wholly be answered to complete satisfaction, neither in an esoteric or mundane state.

As I see it, religion was created by man to control others for greed and power. What I think most leaders or originators of the world's main religions actually set out to do was simplify existing dogma and create a way of life that could be lived more easily.

For instance, Jesus is credited as saying, "the law is summed up in these, Love the Lord you God and love your neighbor as yourself".

Now if that is true then that simple sentence took the place of hundreds of Mosaic and Jewish laws...used to explain the totality of the Ten Commandments. If humankind were to just heed those ten, it would be good, but Jesus made it even more profound...Love one another.

I have said this before, in Being Fear-Free. You have to be able to understand that you must care for yourself.

Love in this case, to me, means respecting and honoring who and what you are, thus you are able to see and assist others in finding that wholeness in themselves.

Look at those around you and see if you accept them as they are? Do you know that they accept themselves as they are? You don't have to ask, if you don't know, then chances are they do not.

There is a soft and gentle confidence which exudes from someone who is in touch with the "real" person inside and how they accept themselves is shown in actions and words.

Living a life of balance is easier than most people think. The edicts and rules and laws blah, blah, blah, all are there in place to direct those who do not live by a code which emanates from within, guiding them to do what is best for themselves and others. That is why criminals exist…they do what they want for themselves only, very selfish!

Balance comes from doing even the simplest task with the intention of creating an outcome of balance.

We all know when we do something that is against the rules. There is something inside each of us that hits us in the gut and says, "You really shouldn't be doing this!" as opposed to the feeling of peacefulness when we are engaged in an act of kindness.
Everyone knows it, everyone feels it!

Excuses are used to try and lie your way out of a situation you created with adverse consequences.

Keeping balance - in mind - before you act, will change things significantly!!!

What you say and what you do are signals as to how you perceive yourself and how to accept those perceptions…good, bad, or indifferent.

There are things in all our lives we wish we had not done. There are things we wish we could do over. There are things we wish we could just do! There are things we will never do; things we should never do; things we can never do.

And that is ALL right!!!

Here we are…in a place of being able to understand the universe and all things in it, yet we fuss about the little things, and they're all little things!

Do you wonder what life will be tomorrow or later today? Do you contemplate on the propositions which have come your way and you did not act on them? Do you seek for things that are not wholly within your reach at this time?

I would never say, "Don't try", but I will tell you that you should look at your interests, your passions, and create a road (a path of life) that will lead you in that direction.

It will take time and you may have to redirect your steps from time to time, but be real with yourself and talk to others.

Don't look at starting at the top, just start with what you like and build from there. Remember the guy that created facebook? He only wanted to start a social network for himself and his buddies, but when he started truly creating…it became bigger than he ever thought it could.

He started with passion; an answer born out of a need was established and now the world knows all about it. We embraced the concept and we found ourselves fulfilled by this product/service.

The guy that began this IS now at the top…but he started simple, with a passion and a cause.

Explanation

What has any of this to do with saying something to an ugly baby???

Any baby for that matter…!

Everything! Because this is how we think and how we act and how we judge others and our self. We have to become conscious of the inner mechanisms that give birth to the realities of what we do and what/how we say things.

We have to know:

Think before you speak.

Say something Believable.

Relive your humiliation

(so as not to repeat it)

Speak your Truth about a thing - anything

Keep the Balance

It is far simpler to tell the truth than even try to make up a lie and use it. Each time we use our delightfully creative and innovative minds in imagining a story that we think might get us through a situation, is usually the time when we are caught in a lie! So just tell the truth.

I agree that the truth may need to be provided with a taste of honey, but you should now see the difference between an out-n-out lie, and something that needs to be said in a more candid way.

There is, of course, the times when straight –forward- truth-telling- talk- it- out, is absolutely necessary. We really do live in a world of "shades of grey."

What would you say to an ugly baby… "Yes, I love it, too!!!"

Gratitude:

If you have found this book helpful, or not…please let me know. Feedback is important.

Maybe you have something you need to say, discuss, rave about, or preach on. Share with me. I love people, ideas and the process of learning.

Thank you so much for reading this.

Kindest regards to you,

Gary

garykwright1951@yahoo.com

www.ingramcontent.com/pod-product-compliance
Ingram Content Group UK Ltd.
Pitfield, Milton Keynes, MK11 3LW, UK
UKHW041905190726
13854UKWH00003B/1090